Wetland Animals

Mallards

by Margaret Hall

Consulting Editor: Gail Saunders-Smith, Ph.D.
Consultant: Charlie Luthin, Executive Director
Wisconsin Wetlands Association, Madison, Wisconsin

Capstone
press

Mankato, Minnesota

Pebble Books are published by Capstone Press
151 Good Counsel Drive, P.O. Box 669, Mankato, Minnesota 56002
http://www.capstonepress.com

1 2 3 4 5 6 09 08 07 06 05 04

Library of Congress Cataloging-in-Publication Data
Hall, Margaret, 1947–
    Mallards/by Margaret Hall.
    p. cm.—(Wetland animals)
    Summary: Photographs and simple text introduce the characteristics and
behavior of mallard ducks.
    Includes bibliographical references and index.
    ISBN 0-7368-2065-5 (hardcover)
    1. Mallard—Juvenile literature. [1. Mallard. 2. Ducks.] I. Title. II. Series.
QL696.A52 H328 2004
598.4'134—dc21   2003008555

Note to Parents and Teachers

The Wetland Animals series supports national science standards
related to life science. This book describes and illustrates mallards.
The photographs support early readers in understanding the text.
The repetition of words and phrases helps early readers learn new
words. This book also introduces early readers to subject-specific
vocabulary words, which are defined in the Glossary section. Early
readers may need assistance to read some words and to use the
Table of Contents, Glossary, Read More, Internet Sites, and
Index/Word List sections of the book.

Table of Contents

Mallards

Mallards are ducks.
Ducks are waterbirds
with wings, feathers,
and webbed feet.

Male mallards have green, white, and brown feathers. Female mallards have mostly brown feathers.

Mallards have short necks and flat bills.

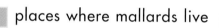

places where mallards live

Wetlands

Mallards live in many wetlands around the world. Wetlands are areas of land covered by water and plants.

What Mallards Do

Mallards swim in lakes, ponds, streams, and rivers.

Mallards dip their heads under the water to find food.

Mallards eat mostly plants and seeds. They sometimes eat insects and snails.

Mallards build nests
in grass or reeds near
the water. Female
mallards lay eggs
and raise ducklings.

Flying

Mallards fly to warm places in winter.

Glossary

bill—the hard part of a bird's mouth

feather—a light, fluffy part that covers a bird's body; a male mallard's feathers are brighter than a female mallard's feathers.

nest—a home of sticks or grass that birds build; birds lay their eggs and raise their young in nests; mallards build their nests close to water.

reed—a tall hollow plant that grows in wetlands

webbed—having folded skin or tissue between an animal's toes or fingers; ducks have webbed feet to help them swim better.

wetland—an area of land that is covered by water and plants; marshes, swamps, and bogs are wetlands.

Read More

Lindeen, Carol K. *Life in a Wetland.* Pebble Plus: Living in a Biome. Mankato, Minn.: Capstone Press, 2004.

Mitchell, Melanie S. *Ducks.* Life Cycles. Minneapolis: Lerner Publications, 2003.

Morgan, Sally. *Ducks and Other Birds.* Life Cycles. North Mankato, Minn.: Thameside Press, 2001.

Internet Sites

FactHound offers a safe, fun way to find Internet sites related to this book. All of the sites on FactHound have been researched by our staff.

Here's how:
1. Visit *www.facthound.com*
2. Type in this special code **0736820655** for age-appropriate sites. Or enter a search word related to this book for a more general search.
3. Click on the Fetch It button.

FactHound will fetch the best sites for you!

23

Index/Word List

bills, 9
build, 19
ducklings, 19
ducks, 5
eat, 17
eggs, 19
feathers, 5, 7
feet, 5

female, 7, 19
fly, 21
food, 15
live, 11
male, 7
nests, 19
plants, 11, 17
raise, 19

reeds, 19
swim, 13
warm, 21
waterbirds, 5
webbed, 5
wetlands, 11
wings, 5
winter, 21

Word Count: 105
Early-Intervention Level: 13

Editorial Credits
Sarah L. Schuette, editor; Patrick Dentinger, series designer; Scott Thoms,
photo researcher; Karen Risch, product planning editor

Photo Credits
Brian Gosewisch, 6
Corbis, 14
Corel, 10
Index Stock Imagery/Robert Franz, 8
Kit Breen, 16
McDonald Wildlife Photography/Joe McDonald, cover
Richard Hamilton Smith, 12
Stockbyte, 1
Tom & Pat Leeson, 4, 18
Tom Stack & Associates/Thomas Kitchin, 20